FIVE 5 FINGER PIANO

BEATLES! BEATLES!

T0061031

ISBN 978-0-7935-3512-5

HAL•LEONARD™
CORPORATION
7777 W. BLUEMOUND RD. P.O. BOX 13819 MILWAUKEE, WI 53213

Copyright © 1994 by HAL LEONARD CORPORATION
International Copyright Secured   All Rights Reserved

A Hard Day's Night

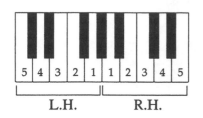

L.H.   R.H.

Words and Music by John Lennon
and Paul McCartney

Driving

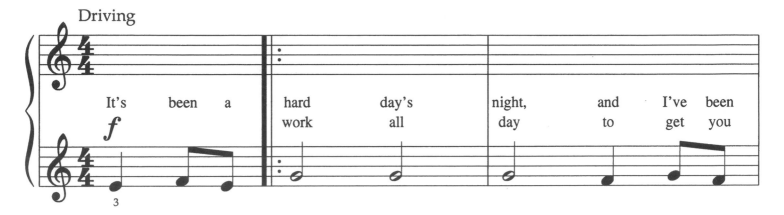

It's been a | hard day's | night, and I've been
work all | day to | get you

work — ing like a | dog. _____ It's been a | hard day's
mon — ey to buy you | things. _____ And it's | worth it just to hear you

Duet Part (Student plays one octave higher.)

Driving

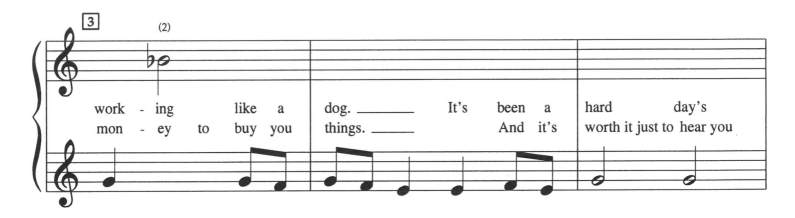

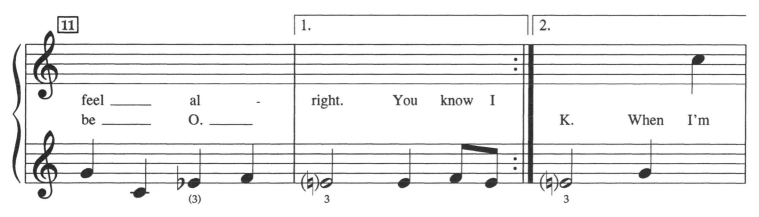

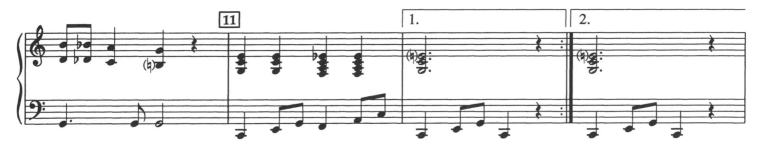

home ev - 'ry - thing seems to be al - right.

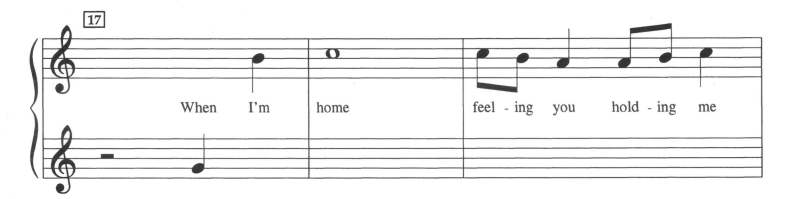

When I'm home feel - ing you hold - ing me

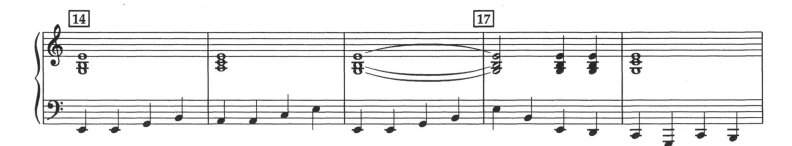

tight, tight. Yeah, it's been a hard day's

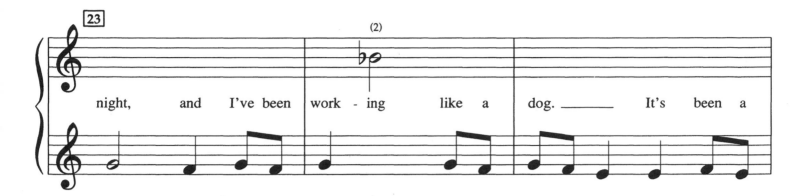

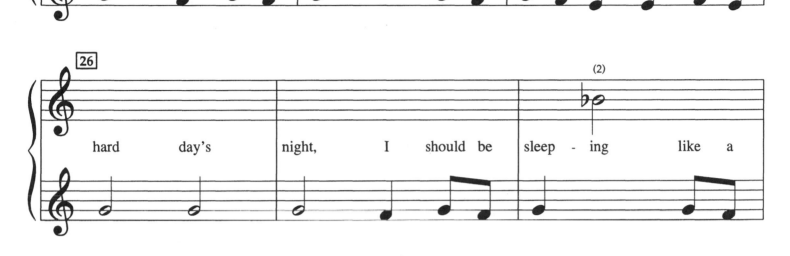

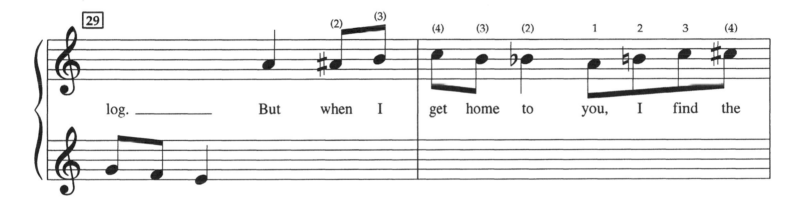

thing that you do will make me feel _____ al -

right. You know I feel _____ al -

right. You know I feel al - right.

Hey Jude

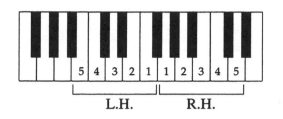

Words and Music by John Lennon
and Paul McCartney

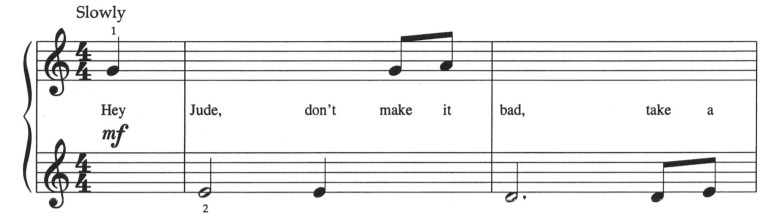

Slowly

Hey Jude, don't make it bad, take a

mf

sad song and make it bet - ter. _____ Re - mem - ber to let her into your

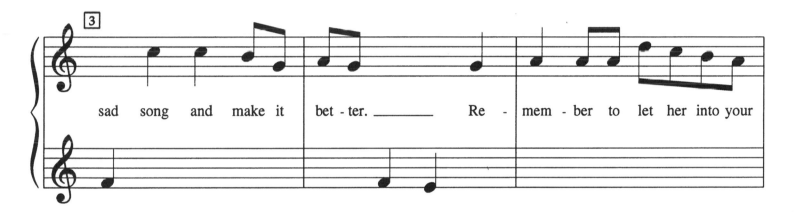

Duet Part (Student plays one octave higher.)

Slowly

mp

With pedal

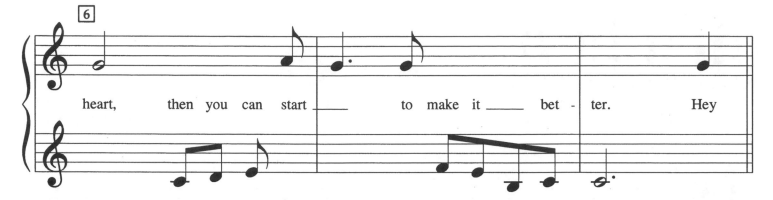

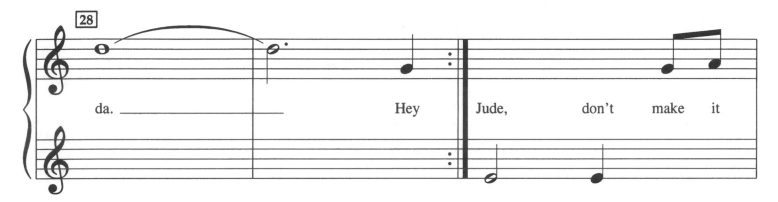

mem - ber to let her under your skin, then you'll be - gin _____ to make it

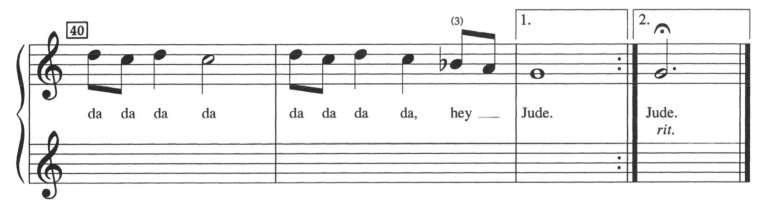

bet -ter, bet -ter, bet -ter, bet -ter, bet -ter bet -ter, oh! Da da da

da da da da da da da da, hey ___ Jude. Jude.
rit.

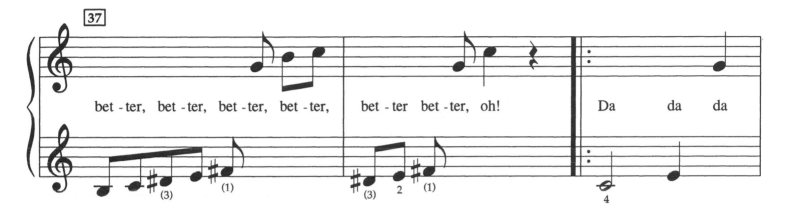

Love Me Do

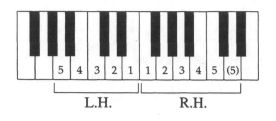

Words and Music by John Lennon
and Paul McCartney

With a bounce

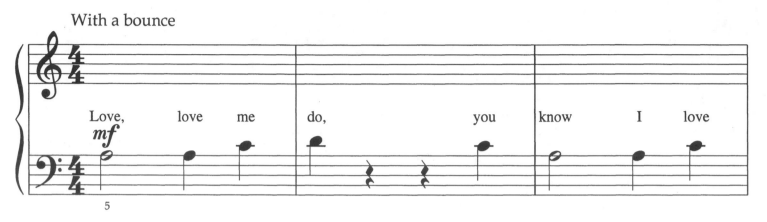

Love, love me do, you know I love

you, I'll al - ways be true, so please _____

Duet Part (Student plays one octave higher.)
With a bounce

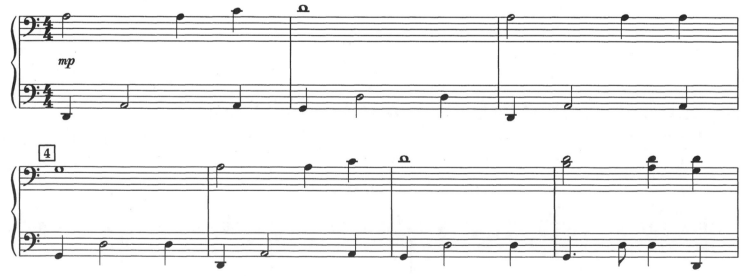

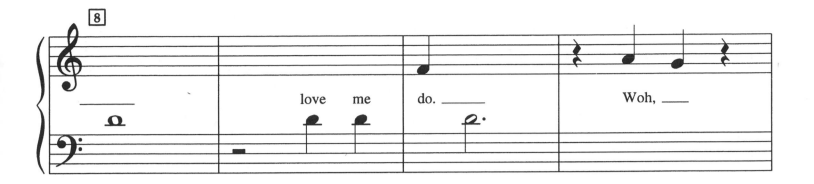

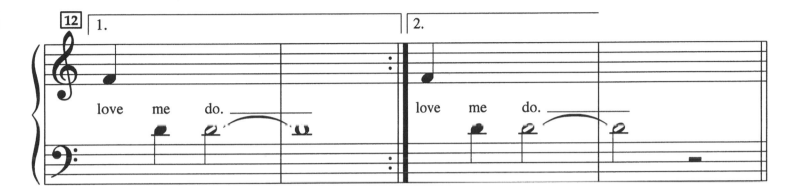

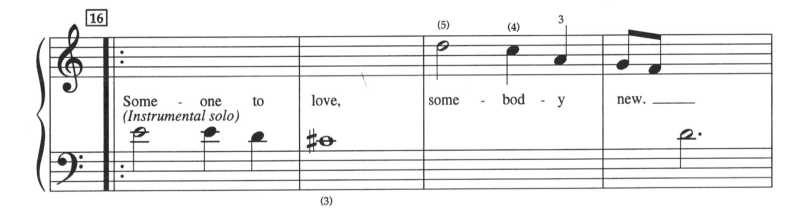

15

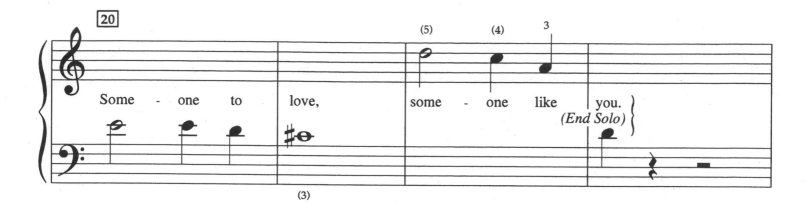

Some - one to love, some - one like you. *(End Solo)*

Love, love me do, you know I love

you, I'll al - ways be true, so please _____

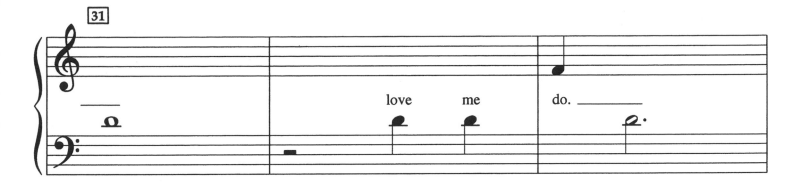

17

P.S. I Love You

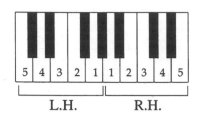

Words and Music by John Lennon
and Paul McCartney

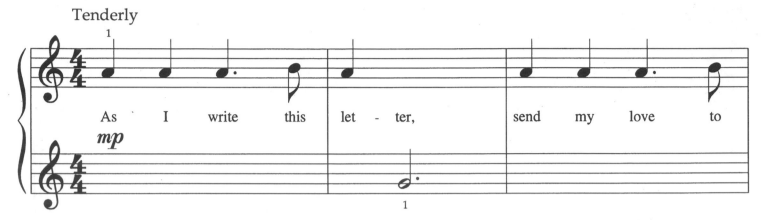

As I write this let - ter, send my love to

you, re - mem - ber that I'll al - ways

Duet Part (Student plays one octave lower.)

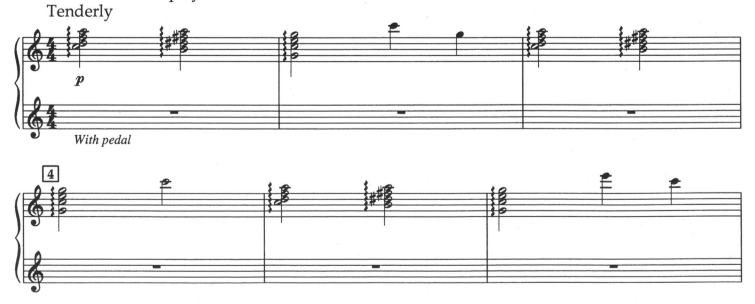

be in love with ___ you. Treas - ure these few

words till we're to - geth - er, keep all my love for -

ev - er. P. S. I love you, _____

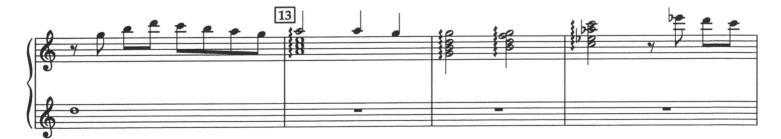

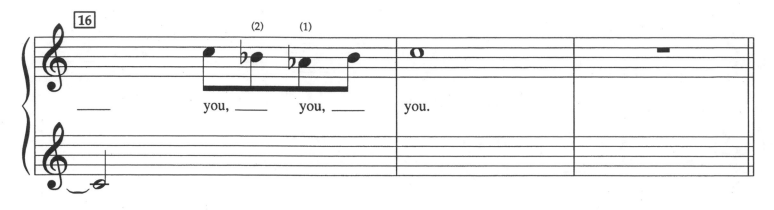

you, _____ you, _____ you.

(1., D.S.) I'll be com - ing home a - gain to you love and
(2.) Treas - ure these few words till we're to - geth - er, and keep

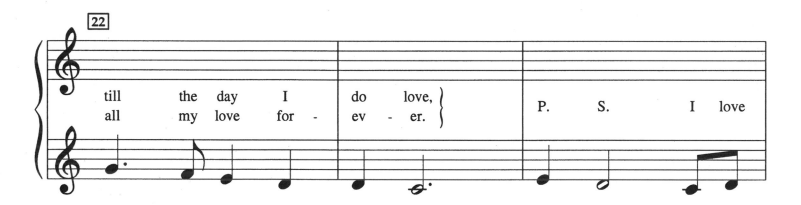

till the day I do love,
all my love for - ev - er. } P. S. I love

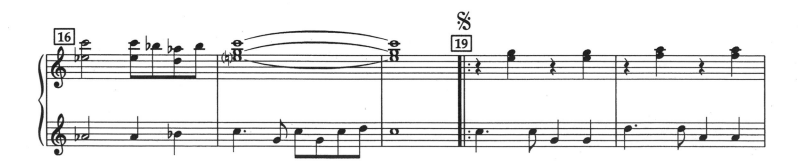

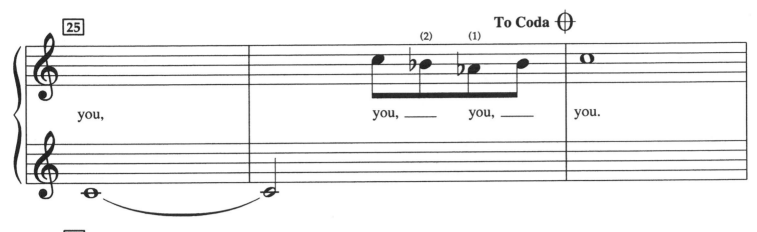

you,

you, _____ you, _____ you.

As I write this let - ter,

send my love to you, re - mem - ber that I'll

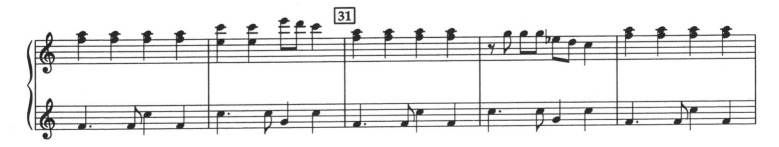

21

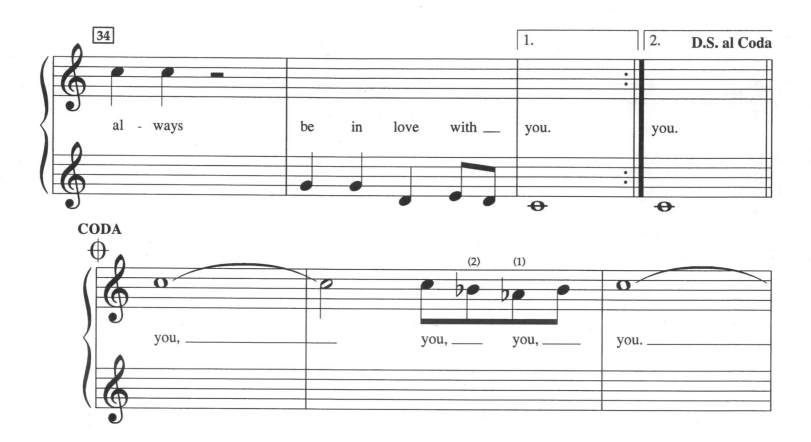

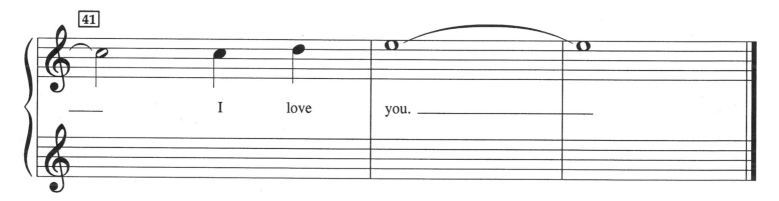

Yesterday

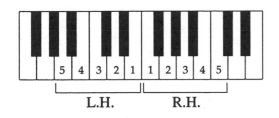

Words and Music by John Lennon
and Paul McCartney

With expression

Yes - ter - day,
Sud - den - ly,

all my troub - les seemed so
I'm not half the man I

far a - way.
used to be.

Now it looks as though they're
There's a shad - ow hang - ing

Duet Part (Student plays one octave higher.)

With expression

With pedal

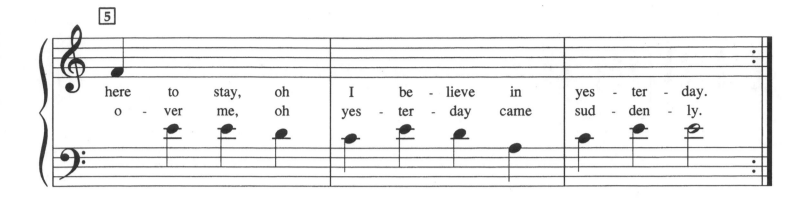

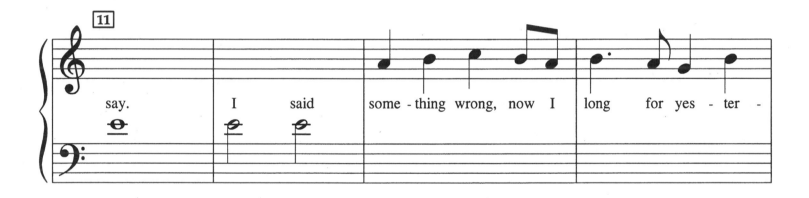

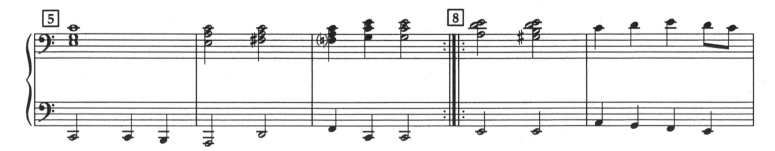

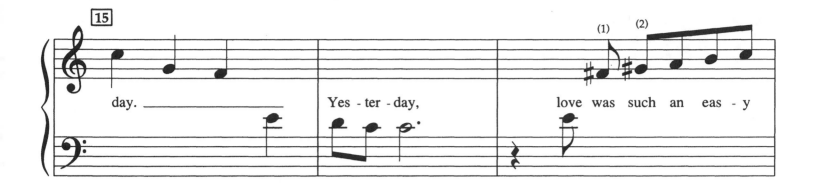

day. _____ Yes-ter-day, love was such an eas-y

game to play. Now I need a place to hide a-way, oh

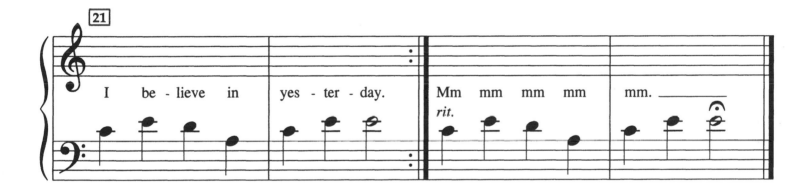

I be-lieve in yes-ter-day. Mm mm mm mm mm. _____

Ticket To Ride

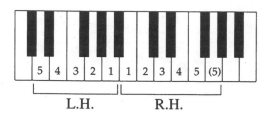

Words and Music by John Lennon
and Paul McCartney

Duet Part (Student plays one octave higher.)

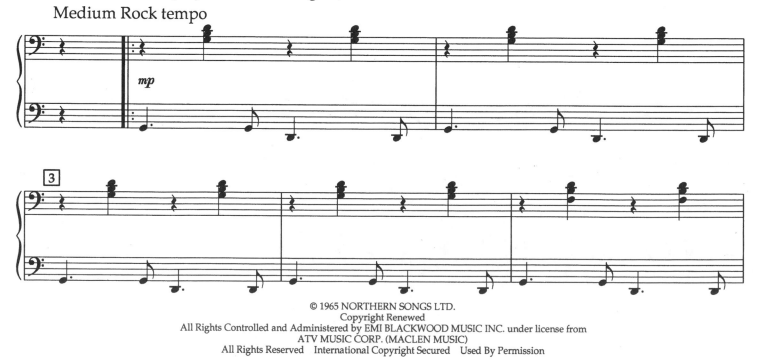

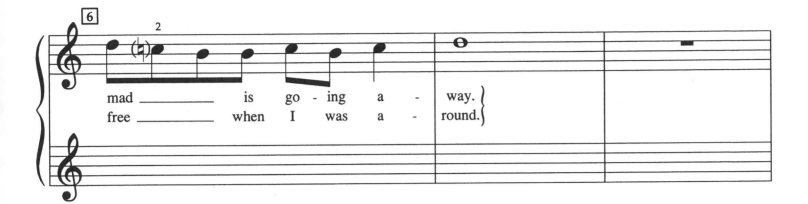

mad _____ is go - ing a - way.
free _____ when I was a - round.

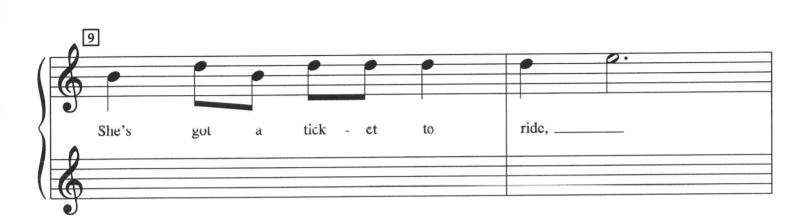

She's got a tick - et to ride, _____

she's got a tick - et to ri - hi - hide,

she's got a tick - et to ride, but she don't

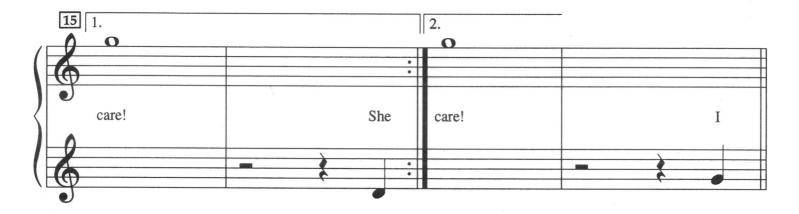

care! She care! I

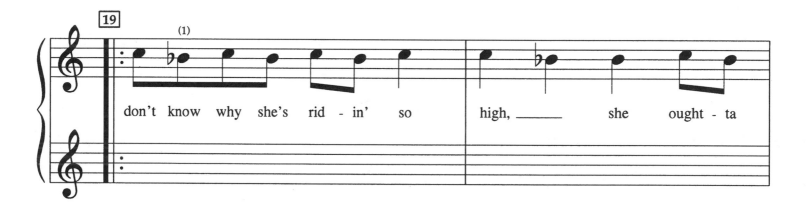

don't know why she's rid - in' so high, _____ she ought - ta

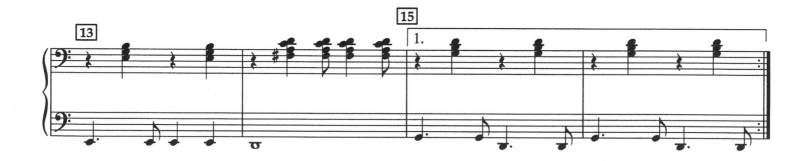

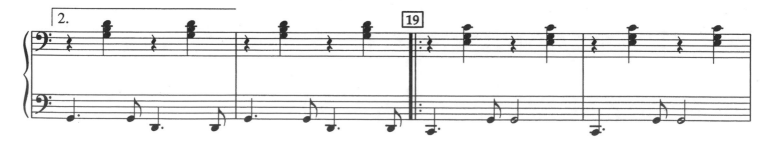

think twice, she oughtta do right by me. Be -

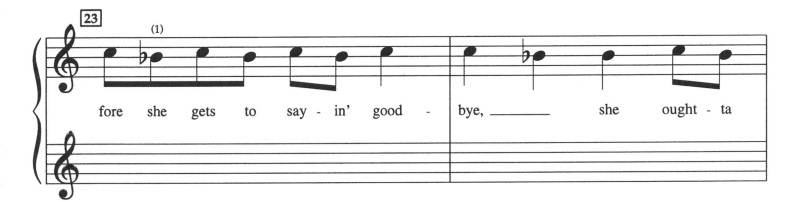

fore she gets to say - in' good - bye, _____ she ought - ta

think twice, she oughtta do right by me.

29

I think I'm gon - na be sad, I think it's to -
She said that liv - ing with me is bring - in' her

day yeah! ___ The girl that's driv - ing me
down yeah! ___ For she would nev - er be

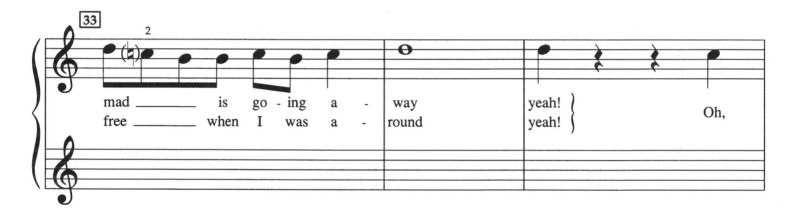

mad ___ is go - ing a - way yeah! Oh,
free ___ when I was a - round yeah!

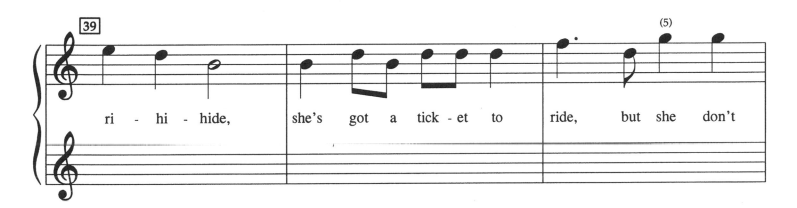

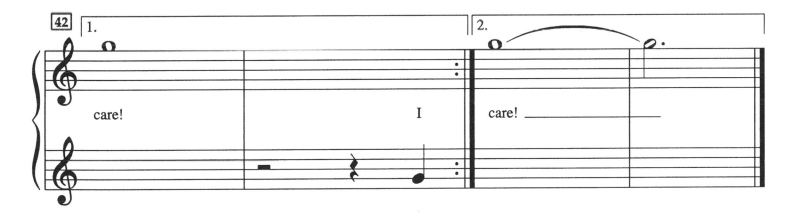

Twist And Shout

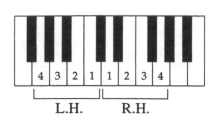

Words and Music by Bert Russell
and Phil Medley

With a twist

Well, shake it up, ba - by __ now, twist and

shout. Come on, come on, come on, come on, ba - by __ now,

Duet Part (Student plays one octave higher.)

With a twist

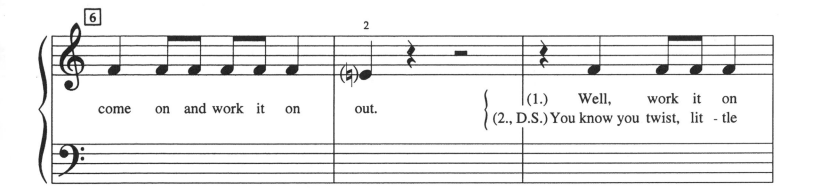

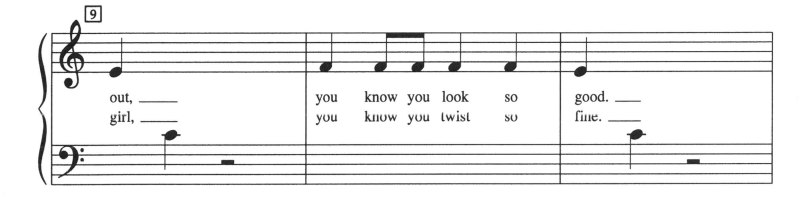

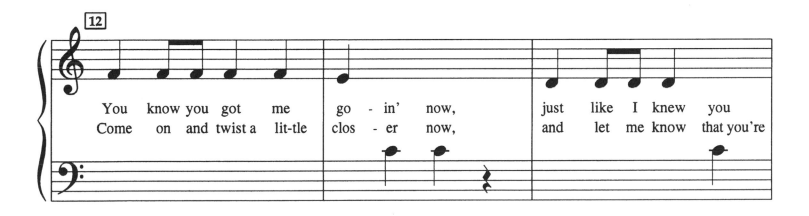

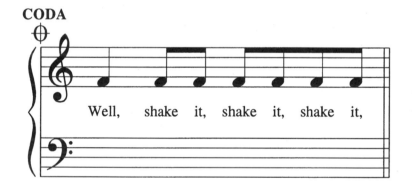

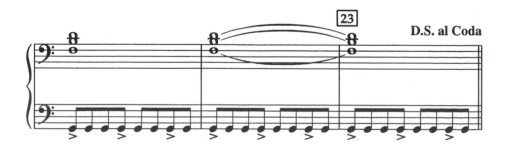

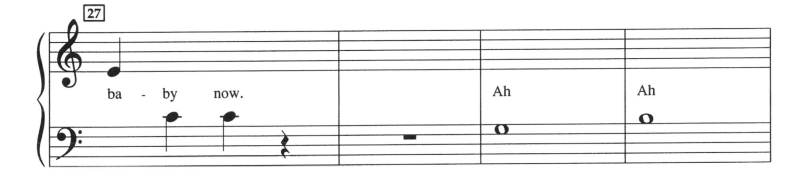

Yellow Submarine

Words and Music by John Lennon
and Paul McCartney

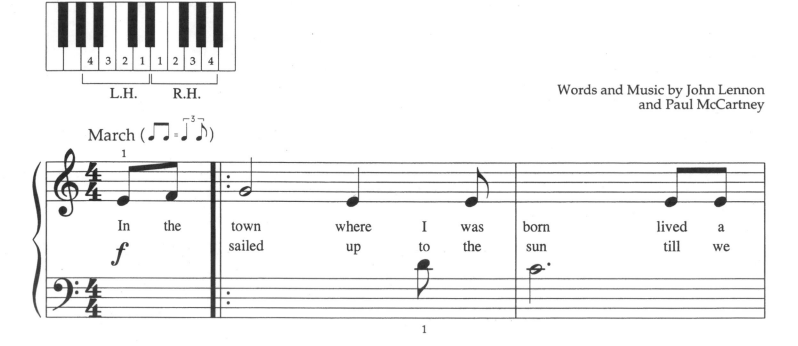

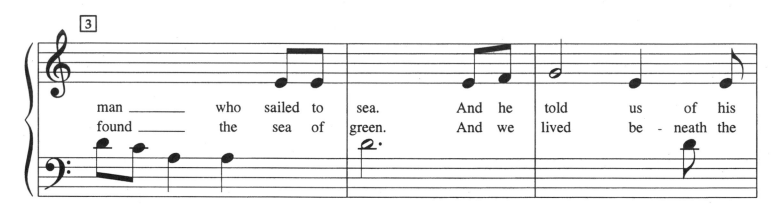

Duet Part (Student plays one octave higher.)

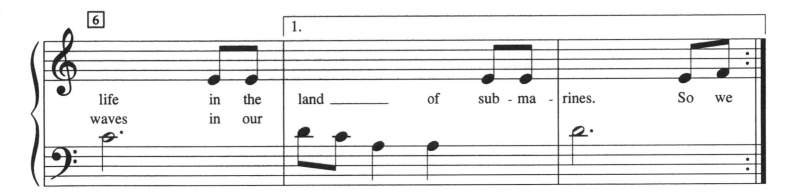

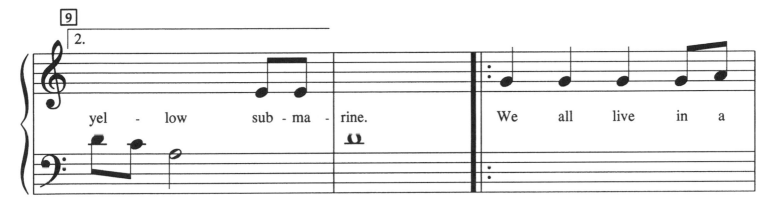

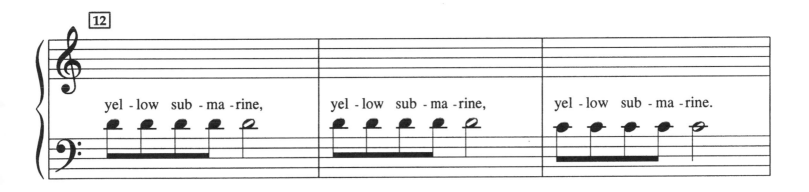

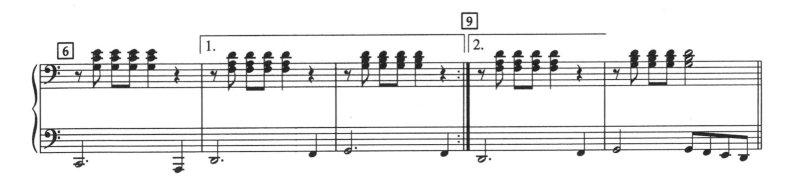

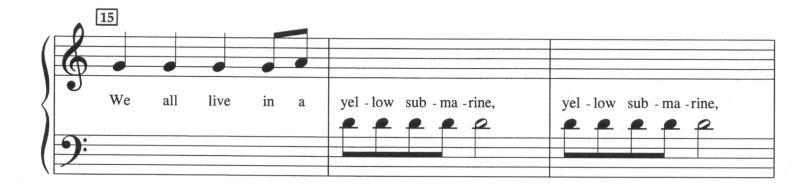

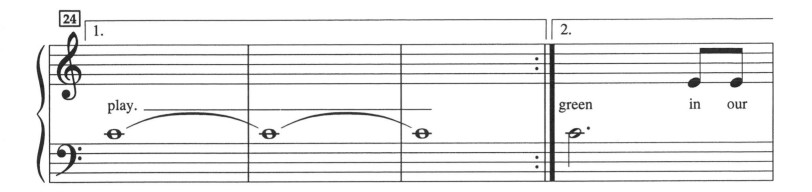

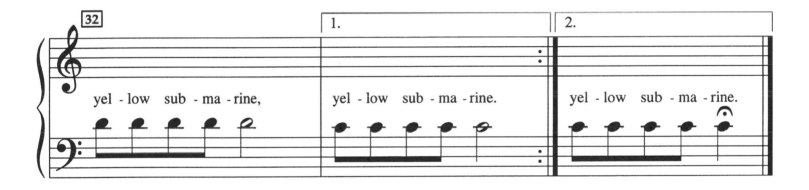

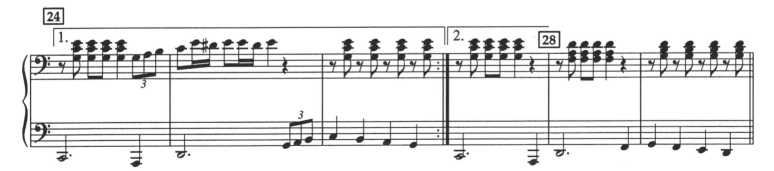

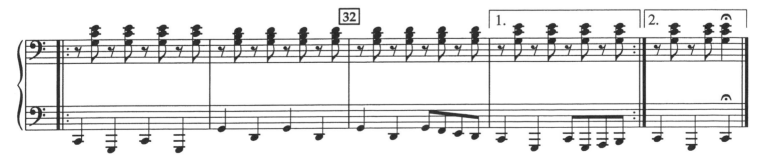